HAUNTED

SALEM

&

BEYOND

HAUNTED SALEM & BEYOND

ISBN 0-9700718-3-3

All photos taken by the author unless otherwise noted.

Book cover by Jo Butz, *Graphic Design Studio.*

Back cover graphic by *CatStuff.*

Printed on recycled paper by *Sheridan Books.*

Cover photo: *Statue of Roger Conant in Salem Square.*

CONTENTS

INTRODUCTION

Salem, Massachusetts is one of America's oldest and most mysterious seaports harboring *more* than its share of ghosts.

Her sheltered and fertile land attracted Roger Conant and a small group of pioneers away from rocky, stormy Cape Ann in 1626. They called the small colony *Naumkeag* meaning "comfort haven."

The notorious witch trials play a part in the ghostly mayhem occurring in the harbor town, but the city's rich history consists of much more than the dark times.

Salem was a leader in colonial settlement, the struggle for independence, international trade, and the birth of industrialization.

The Maritime History of Massachusetts by Samuel Eliot Morison paints a picture of the city in its heyday:

"Salem with a little under eight thousand inhabitants, was the sixth largest city in the United States in 1790. Her appearance was more antique than even that of Boston, and her reek of salt water, that almost surrounded her, yet more pronounced.

For half a mile along the harbor front, subtended by the long finger of Derby Wharf, ran Derby Street, the residential and business center of the town.

On one side were the houses of the gentry, Derbys and Princes, and Crownshields, goodly gambrel or hip-roofed brick and wooden mansions dating from the middle of the century, standing well back with tidy gardens in front.

Opposite were the wharves, separated from the street by counting rooms, warehouses, ship-chandler' stores, pump-makers' shops, sailmakers' lofts; all against a background of spars, rigging, and furled or brailed-up sails.

Crowded within three hundred years of Derby Street, peeping between the merchants' mansions and over their garden walls like small boys behind a police cordon, were some eighteen or nineteen hundred buildings, including dwellings of pre-witch-craft days, with overhanging upper stories, peaked gables, small-paned windows, and hand rifted clapboards black with age. "

Many of the houses in the McIntire Historic District were once home to aristocrats and sea captains. The elegant architecture reflects wealth and affluence. These beloved homes still house some of their former residents, their wraiths refuse to leave – who can blame them?

But not all of Salem's spirits are earth bound. Using her phantom populace as a barometer, the expression *"Old Salts never die, they simply fade away,"* is not totally accurate. Some seafarers do fade, but here in Salem, they haven't exactly gone away – their shades still sail the high seas on schooners and cruisers.

Pirates hold a place in the region's history. Their misdeeds are legendary - their victims' screams still audible.

Native son, Nathaniel Hawthorne penned his penchant for the paranormal in his writings, preserving the haunted history of his day. No less than four of the locations he frequented are lively with the long dead.

The specters of the slaves who passed through Salem and other North Shore stops on the Underground Railroad stay behind adding to the blend of the unique, and almost unbelievable tales that make up *Haunted Salem & Beyond.*

*In the town center, a statue of Salem's founder,
Roger Conant, surveys the settlement.*

SALEM'S WITCH TRIALS

Boredom and bitterness triggered the hysteria in Salem Village in 1692. The small colony of 500 was suffering an atmosphere of political tension, personal feuds, and repressive puritanical practices. What began in harmony had deteriorated into disputes and dissent.

One visitor from Boston described the people as *"savagely vicious"* in their dealings with one another and *"acted more out of jealously and greed than any sense of religious purpose."*

The time was ripe for young girls with wild imaginations. Stirred by tales told by Tituba, a West Indian slave, bizarre behavior, combined with vile accusations, propelled the village into a downward spiral of fear, recrimination, and disastrous loss.

Reverend Samuel Parris' daughter Elizabeth and her cousin Abigail started acting strange. They began to bark like dogs and throw themselves to the ground. For all appearances, they were having fits. One of them even tried to crawl into the fireplace!

A medical examination was arranged, and Dr. Griggs diagnosed the girls with "bewitchment," for which he had no cure.

Soon, other children began to imitate the unusual behavior. One girl even claimed the Devil was after her. The Devil in Salem? Unthinkable! The evil must be stopped! At a town meeting, the populace pledged to seek out and destroy the individuals bewitching the young people.

Children pointed the finger at certain villagers and claimed their "spirits" had cast spells upon them. The targeted unfortunates were out of favor, or considered unconventional, by the pompous "powers that be" in the community.

One third of the residents of Salem Village were falsely charged, publicly slandered, and locked away in a dark, damp, dirty dungeon. Yes, the Devil *had* anchored in Salem. For those accused, this *was* hell.

When Governor William Phipps' wife was maligned, he ended the madness, and liberated 168, by stating that "spectral evidence" was not allowed.

After all was said and done, one hundred and fifty-six people were indicted, nineteen were hanged, and one man was pressed to death. Even two dogs were hanged, charged with giving the children the "evil eye."

CURSE OF GILES COREY

The Essex High Sheriff, George Corwin, was a ne'er do well who was fortunate to have a well-connected Judge for a father. To insure his son's success, witch trial Judge Jonathan Corwin made certain his son obtained the prestigious post.

Corwin was a vicious man who secured his place in Salem's history during those awful thirteen months with the cruelest of all his misdeeds - the crushing death of octogenarian Giles Corey.

Corey refused to plead one way or another (those who pleaded guilty were set free since nobody wanted to find out what would happen if you killed a real witch!) His wife had already been convicted of witchery and hung on Gallows Hill. He stayed silent.

The High Sheriff justified his abusive plan by using an ancient English law that allowed the crushing of suspected warlocks if they remained mute as Corey did.

Giles Corey was stripped naked and publicly taken to an open field behind the present site of the Old Jail. He was laid down in a shallow hole in the ground, a heavy board placed on top of his body and one by one large boulders were placed on him. The weight of the stones was supposed to *crush* the truth out of Corey, but the man kept silent.

An eyewitness to the torture, Robert Calef wrote: *"In the crushing, Giles Corey's tongue was pressed out of his mouth, and the Sheriff, with his cane, forced it in again."*

As a result of the inhumane torture the man succumbed. His dying words were: *"Damn you. I curse you and Salem!"*

The thieving, evil Sheriff Corwin, who confiscated the possessions and property of many of the accused as his, own, died in 1696 of a heart attack.

Since that day, Essex County's Sheriffs stationed at the Salem Jail near the open field where Corey was crushed, seem to have suffered Giles Corey curse – *every one of them either died in office of a heart attack or was forced to retire because of a heart condition or blood ailment!*

HOWARD STREET BURYING GOUND

Howard Street is known as *"the most haunted street in Salem."* (Of course it helps that the street runs right next to the cemetery.) The Burying Ground is located behind the remnants of the nightmarish Old Jail built during the War of 1812. Supposedly, the phantoms of those once imprisoned there continue doing time in the afterlife.

Legend says the sighting of the disembodied spirit of Giles Corey near the stronghold signals adversity for the small community. To put it in Nathaniel Hawthorne's words: *"the ghost of the wizard appears as a precursor of some calamity impending over the community."*

Such was the case when Corey made an appearance shortly before the great fire that swept through Salem in 1914. Ironically, the inferno began at Gallows Hill, destroyed one third of the city, but miraculously left the treasured dwellings of the McIntire Historic District intact.

Sensitives feel a palpable sadness in the area and some claim to have felt icy fingers touch their neck while visiting this distressing spot.

TOWN MEETING HOUSE

The Salem witch trial lasted for thirteen months in what was once known as Salem Village and is now the town of Danvers. When the accusers pointed the finger at Governor William Phipps' wife, the uproar was finally discredited as a form of mass hysteria. Be that as it may, *actual supernatural activity* may have contributed to the paranoia that resulted in the accusations being taken seriously in the first place.

At the trial of Bridget Bishop on March 24, 1692, many witnesses testified that as she was taken under guard past the town meeting house, a poltergeist attack took place:

> *"A Demon invisibly entering the Meeting House, tore down a part of it; so tho' there was no person to be seen, yet the people, at the noise, running in, found a Board which was strongly fastened with several Nails, transported into another quarter of the House."*

WITCH DUNGEON MUSEUM
16 Lynde Street

The Witch Dungeon Museum is a recreation of the original 17th century hellhole. After watching a scene from the trial of Sara Good, visitors are taken into the sobering dungeon. One can only imagine the horrific conditions in 1692 with no heat, no light, and no sanitation. The creepy atmosphere promotes the theory that the cellar is haunted...

...The museum building is a former church and visitors and employees have witnessed the apparition of a hooded monk. The holy man's wraith is most often seen near the "Crushing Death of Giles Corey" recreation. Visit this place and prepare to be chilled!

*The Joshua Ward House was built on the foundation
of cruel High Sheriff George Corwin's home.*

JOSHUA WARD HOUSE
148 Washington Street

By 1790, Salem was a flourishing commercial center and had the *richest* per capita in the country. International trade with Africa, China, Europe, Russia, and the West Indies produced great wealth and prosperity.

Joshua Ward was a successful maritime merchant and sea captain. Originally the house had a view of the South River, but in 1830 the waterway was filled in; now the structure overlooks a plaza.

The Colonial house stood vacant for many years, but thanks to Salem's urban renewal, the old brick house was brought back to life. The restoration apparently revived some long dead inhabitants as well.

Soon after the house was restored, Richard Carlson bought the building and operated Carlson Realty in the historic house. Many haunting incidents began to occur - mostly playful pranks - chairs, lampshades, trashcans, and candlesticks would Be found turned upside down when the staff arrived in the morning. Papers were strewn on the floor and candles, removed from their holders and bent in the shape of an *S*, were found lying on the fireplace.

One of the offices stays ice cold, a classic sign of a ghostly presence.

The security alarms at the office went off over *sixty* times in two years for no explainable reason!

An extraordinary event occurred when Carlson received a call about a particular property plan. Carlson needed to find the plans and call back. No sooner had he hung up the phone *when a rolled up chart came out of the closet of its own accord and spread itself out on the floor in front of Carlson's desk!* This was the document in question! Carlson and a co-worker were eyewitnesses to this spectacular and upsetting event.

No one can be certain who's haunting the 1784 house. The facts we do have is that George Washington really slept here in 1789, and that the venerable home is built on the foundation of George Corwin's house. The placement of the house could be the key to the paranormal activity.

George Corwin was the malicious High Sheriff of Essex County who was responsible for arresting and imprisoning over one hundred and fifty of his neighbors. He interrogated and savored torturing the accused witches in this house. Corwin added insult to injury by confiscating all the victims' possessions after they were hung at Gallows Hill.

When Corwin died shortly after the witch debacle, he was buried in the basement. Because he was so reviled, his family felt the town folk would dig up his corpse and tear him from limb to limb if he was interred in the local graveyard.

Eventually his body was exhumed and moved to the Broad Street Cemetery. Nevertheless, some still feel his evil presence at the site.

Higginson Publishing Company now owns the house, but when it operated as Carlson Realty, one patron witnessed a "weird looking woman" sitting in one of the office chairs and staring off into space. The strange woman was described as having translucent skin and "frizzled" hair, and she was wearing a long gray coat.

The image of this mysterious woman developed on a Polaroid photograph Carlson snapped when taking shots of his employees. The photo reveals one ugly ghost!

Who was this woman and why did she make her presence known? Perhaps she is one of Corwin's victims and stays behind to torment her tormentor.

WONDERFUL, THE WITCH
Nahant

Nahant's "Swallow Cave" was so named because of the large number of swallows that once existed within its cavernous confines.

In 1675 during King Phillip's War, forty Narragansett warriors raided the town of Lynn. The resident men forced the Indians to retreat toward Nahant and the Indians discovered Swallow Cave and hid inside its dark depths.

"Wonderful" was a 17th century witch who lived near Salem. She was an especially intelligent woman who made her living fortune telling — she was exceptionally adept at finding lost property and predicting coming events.

The 70-year-old witch helped the men of Lynn defeat the forty Narragansett Indians. She accurately reported that they were hiding in Swallow Cave ready to attack with their sharp hatchets.

Wonderful's misty apparition appears among the rocks at Swallow Cave during the day and night, but she is most often seen at dusk near the mouth of the cave.

WITCH HOLLOW FARM
474 Ipswich Road, Boxford

This beautiful colonial farmhouse has a long history as a haunted place. Arthur Pinkham, grandson of Lydia Pinkham the inventor of the legendary "women's tonic," was president of his grandmother's company based in Lynn for 30 years and his residence was the 1666 Witch Hollow Farm.

The ghostly activity here is attributed to Mary Tyler who was accused of being a witch during the trouble in 1692. Although innocent, she confessed and was not hanged. Why is a house in Boxford haunted by a woman charged with practicing witchcraft in Salem? The answer is that Mary lived in the house before she married.

Pinkham was fascinated by his resident ghost and documented his recurrent sightings of her phantom. He spoke often and wrote at length about her ghost in his autobiography.

For most of the 1960s, Ed French and his family resided at the Ipswich Road farmhouse. On moonlit nights, Ed was astonished to see Mary walk from the carriage house to the main house.

Other owners also felt that they were not alone. One daughter in particular had the most experiences with the unseen. Once someone called her by name and many times when approaching her bedroom a greenish light was seen glowing within (the French family also saw a green light in that room). When she opened the door, the light was gone.

She and her friend heard the cupboard doors slamming and banging in the kitchen and when they went to investigate the noises stopped. When they went back into the living room the fire in the fireplace was blazing wildly and the room was full of smoke.

Today the Morris family resides at Witch Hollow Farm. They haven't met up with Mary Tyler or any other ghost for that matter. Morris has spoken with former owners who admit they had encounters, but he says in order to live with their family the ghosts would have to have a sense of humor.

HOUSE OF SEVEN GABLES
54 Turner Street

Salem's favorite son Nathaniel Hawthorne is a central figure in the town's haunted history. Hawthorne had first hand knowledge of those on the other side and the novelist seems to have been a magnet for the supernatural. Four locations the author frequented are reputedly lively with spirits.

The gabled house is not only one of Salem's most notable structures, but one of America's. The historic waterside complex is a national historic *district* comprised of six houses, and includes the dark clapboard 1668 house that inspired Hawthorne's romance novel, as well as his birthplace.

Nathaniel Hawthorne was born in Salem on July 4, 1804 and a dressmaker's ghost possesses the house where he was born. Her spirit has been seen sewing and walking in the house.

The House of Seven Gables was originally the Turner-Ingersoll Mansion. Hawthorne, descendant of one of the witchcraft judges, lived in the fabled home with his cousin Susan Ingersoll. Hawthorne was certain the place was haunted and put these notions on paper in his famous novel.

The House of Seven Gables – Nathaniel Hawthorne's haunting impressions were on the mark.

Many of the guides who work at one of New England's oldest surviving 17th century wooden mansions, concur with Hawthorne. Ancestral portraits adorn the walls and the eyes of those depicted seem to follow their every move.

Susan Ingersoll died in the house when she was 72 years old and her phantom is said to put in appearances from time to time in her former abode.

The house was a stop on the Underground Railroad and its hiding places include a secret staircase, hidden closets, and large dark storage area.

Strange sounds reverberate throughout and are attributed to the revenants of the slaves who stayed there. Some of the inexplicable occurrences are toilets flushing, faucets flowing, door latches lifting, and doors opening, all on their own.

The specter of a little boy dressed in Victorian clothing has been seen in the attic where the sounds of a child playing and footsteps echo.

Photos taken of the house show spectral visages peering out the windows. It seems that Hawthorne's impressions were on the mark!

Certainly the House of Seven Gables is one of the eeriest in this town full of haunted places.

Unexplainable shadows pervade Salem's U. S. Custom House.

SALEM'S CUSTOM HOUSE

Salem's Custom House is part of the Salem Maritime National Historic Site, the first national historic site in the National Park System. The area is comprised of nine acres and twelve historic structures along the waterfront and the Visitor Center downtown.

The site showcases the development of trade during colonial times, privateering during the American Revolution, and the international maritime trade, particularly with the Far East, which launched America's economic independence after the Revolution.

The imposing 1819 Custom House overlooks Derby Wharf and represented the presence of the United States government in the seaport. Nathaniel Hawthorne worked in the building as an inspector from 1846-1849. Permits to land cargo, seaman's protection and ship's measurement certificates were some of the documents issued there.

Park service employees keep their opinion close to the vest but subtly concur that the edifice harbors the spirits of old salts reliving the good times and feisty sea captains wrangling over custom duties.

FORMULA TO KEEP GHOSTS AWAY

4 ounces water
2 tablespoons salt
1 tablespoon bay laurel (powdered)
4 ounces vinegar
1 tablespoon basil (powdered)
1 teaspoon jalop powder

Mix ingredients together in a large bowl. Place half in a glass by the front door and the other half in a small glass by the back door. Make a second batch of the mixture and sprinkle your entire house as you chant:

Mighty power of this brew,
Exorcise all spirits who
Would haunt, obsess, or me possess.
Send them to a place of rest.
Banish all who would control,
Take them to the place of old
Where they must learn to see the light,
And evermore to do what's right.
Haunting ones from here must go,
Or be ye burned! I say it's so!

SALEM ATHENAEUM

Salem's Athenaeum was a subscription library founded in 1810 to replace two earlier subscription libraries, the Social Library and the Philosophical Library, both of which operated in the 18th century.

Aspiring writer Nathaniel Hawthorne spent each noon away from his duties at the Custom House reading at the austere edifice.

So did 80-year-old Reverend Harris. The library mandated quiet but the two men acknowledged each other's presence daily with a silent nod. The older man sat in the same chair every day reading his paper.

Reverend Harris ultimately passed on and his loss was duly mourned. Hawthorne missed his silent companion, but then a strange thing happened.

For five consecutive days *after his death*, Hawthorne observed the old gentleman sitting in his usual chair by the fireplace reading quietly as he always had.

Hawthorne documented this phenomenon thereby preserving the record of the octogenarian's ghostly appearance for posterity.

The haunted Hawthorne Hotel.

HAWTHORNE HOTEL
On the Common

In the heart of Salem is her traditional New England Common. The neat nine-acre park was at one time used to graze livestock, and in the 17th and 18th centuries, served as a militia training ground.

Today the park is known as Washington Square and is the setting for picnics, games, and concerts.

The handsome Hawthorne Hotel, Salem's tallest building, overlooks the square's activities from her six-story windows. Surrounded by the many grand homes erected by the wealthy sea captains, the Salem Marine Society was founded by the skippers in 1766.

The society's building was razed when the town determined it was time to construct the hotel. As a condition of acquiring the land, the hotel's owners agreed to provide a meeting place for the men.

A small structure whose interior is a replica of the cabin of a barque called the *Taria Topan* was built on the hotel's roof and still serves as headquarters for this exclusive organization.

Some employees wonder if the spirits of some of those old sea captains have returned...

Perhaps the strong personalities of those dogged seafarers are too strong to be extinguished. Some still search for their fellows and seem to be only slightly inconvenienced by the fact that a hotel now stands where once was held convivial meetings.

How else to explain some of the strange incidents reported over the years at the hotel?

Employees and guests alike often noticed that although no one was near, the large ship's wheel used in the nautical décor of the Main Brace Restaurant was turning back and forth as though following a ghostly course. Those who tried to stop the movement found that the wheel seemed to have a mind of its own and would resume its motion.

The Hawthorne retains a nautical theme in its Lower Deck designed to look like a ship's interior. At least one employee refused to work nights in this room after several instances in which he spent considerable time setting up the room only to return moments later to find all the tables and chairs facing in the opposite direction.

And might it be that at least one of the captains likes to keep track of what his successors are doing? Who else can it be disturbing the charts and journals stored in the marine Society's locked roof headquarters?

ROPES MANSION
318 Essex Street

The town's intrepid sea captains helped to make Salem a dominant seaport. Her successful merchants built majestic homes, many of which still stand in the historic McIntire district.

They also established cultural institutions like the Peabody Essex Museum, the nation's oldest continuously operating museum that showcases objects acquired from distant ports in the 17th and 18th centuries.

The Ropes Mansion, just two doors down from the Witch House, is in the heart of the Historic District. Designed by architect-woodcarver Samuel McIntire in the early 1700s, the mansion is one of Salem's finest old homes.

The Ropes family settled in Salem in 1630 and made their fortune in foreign trade.

The Mansion, as it soon became known, was the birthplace of wealthy and influential merchants, writers, attorneys, judges, and sea captains.

The beautiful home made a cameo appearance in the movie *Hocus Pocus* filmed in Salem in 1993.

Do Judge Nathaniel Ropes and his wife Abigail remain in their earthly abode?

An extra room was added to the house solely to display the fine Oriental porcelain that was brought back from trading voyages.

During the Revolution, Judge Nathaniel Ropes lived in the house. Staunchly loyal to the Crown, the Judge's politics agitated a faction of angry colonists. They conjured up a plan to lynch the diehard Tory.

They arrived at the mansion and prepared to abduct the Judge, but Ropes was already on his deathbed; his would-be executioners allowed nature to take its course.

Judge Ropes' wife Abigail also died in the house. Hers was a bizarre and tragic passing.

One night she accidentally passed too close to the fireplace and her nightgown quickly went up in flames. She screamed for help, but no one in the house heard her cries. Abigail burned to death in the upstairs bedroom.

At the turn of the 19th century the property was willed to the Essex Museum along with a cash annuity to maintain the house and gardens in perpetuity. But by the 1970s however, the money was gone and the mansion began to deteriorate.

In 1990 the Peabody-Essex Museum acquired the neglected mansion, and with an influx of new funds, the structure and gardens were restored to their former glory and are now stately and elegant memorials of days gone by.

Gardens are a rarity in Salem, (this was a commercial center, not a farming community), so perhaps that is why a visit to the Mansion's garden is so special. It is a treat to stroll along the pathways and through the arbors; there's a feeling that time has stood still among the formal flowerbeds, flowering shrubs and trees.

More than flora can be found among the plants. On moonlit nights the phantom forms of its former inhabitants can sometimes be seen floating along the manicured paths.

The mansion holds a fine collection of American furniture and decorative arts, as well as the Ropes family books, papers, and personal objects that provide a glimpse into everyday life in the 18th, 19th and early 20th centuries.

Some visitors swear that the apparitions of Judge Ropes and Abigail still roam the halls of their grand house just as they did over two hundred years ago.

Pictures taken of the house's furnishings for insurance purposes reveal an indentation on a sofa indicating that someone is sitting there, *yet nobody can be seen in the photo!*

JOSEPH EDWARDS HOUSE

The three story brick Federal style Joseph Edwards House was built in 1807 and is listed on the National Registry of Historic Places as well as the Massachusetts Historical Directory.

Joseph Edwards was Salem's House Wright when he built the home. He supervised the construction of Salem's Custom House, McIntire's Registry of Deeds building, the Salem Jail and the Jailer's House.

The building has two additions, one constructed in the 1860s to house the kitchen and a bedroom, the other a carriage house put on in the 1930s.

The original house was constructed of wood in 1805/6, but burned to the ground one winter night when the parents left the children home alone. The youngsters were feeding the fire to keep warm when the house went ablaze alighting several neighboring homes that burned to the ground as well.

The present owners were forewarned of the haunting activity by tenants and even had a mystifying experience before they signed the contract to purchase, but they were not deterred.

Bob Barraco was a tenant in the house at one time and wrote about his experiences in the *Ghost Trackers Newsletter*. He and his wife experienced the sound of someone sighing next to them while they were sitting on the couch and *"then the shadow of a partial figure walked by and into the next room."* They heard closet doors open and someone walking upstairs when no body was up there.

One April morning, Barraco was stunned to see *"the specter of an old Spanish gentleman walking around the garden."* According to Barraco, the First Church of Salem owned the house in 1872 and sponsored a Cuban diplomat who was in exile. The Cuban exile eventually died in the house. He and most of his family members are buried in Salem.

In another story by Barraco, he reports that a Federal style house in the vicinity of Salem's historic district harbors haunting activity.

The resident wraith occupied the third floor apartment and seemed to move about as he did when alive. Arriving home, the invisible man would stomp his feet at the front door as if kicking off snow or mud and then walk heavily to the kitchen. His footsteps resounded all about the garret. The unseen presence also liked to sit on the bed and wake up (*and scare!*) whoever was sleeping there.

1801 LACE FACTORY

Claudia Hartford never believed in ghosts until she and her husband purchased a large dilapidated house in Salem. Constructed in 1801, the young energetic couple looked forward to restoring the old building.

Claudia gave birth to their first child and at night when she went into the kitchen to heat the baby's bottle she had the strong sense that someone was watching her. The room was noticeably cold and she detected the aroma of honeysuckle (but there was no sprig of the sweet smelling flower in the area!).

Hartford worked hard restoring the house. He knocked down walls, sawed and hammered. Slowly the couple realized they had disturbed whoever or whatever had been dormant in the vintage dwelling. They were certain they had a ghost.

Many times during the night they were awakened by the sound of glass breaking but they never found any shattered glass.

After some research they learned their house had been a lace factory in the early 1800s and subsequently had been converted into a barn.

On several occasions the couple observed their daughter talking to someone they couldn't see and the little girl also indicated that there was an invisible someone in her closet.

At one time Claudia discerned a shadowy figure dressed in white lace.

The Hartfords eventually sold the house and moved west. On a visit back east they encountered the new owner of the Salem home. Claudia tentatively asked if they had experienced any unusual happenings in the house.

"Oh, you mean the ghost!" was their candid reply. Indeed the resident husband and wife had had several encounters with the lady in lace.

...O'er all there hung the shadows of a fear,
A sense of mystery the spirit daunted,
And said, as plain as whisper in the ear,
The place is Haunted!

From "The Haunted House" by Thomas Hood

EGG ROCK
Nahant

The resort town of Nahant is located just south of Lynn on a peninsula that juts out into the Atlantic.

By 1800s, the town was a tourist mecca. Visitors stayed in boarding houses and private homes until the first hotel was built in 1803.

Off the rocky coast is a massive boulder known as Egg Rock. The rock is a noted landmark and popular destination for pleasure boaters.

In the autumn of 1815, an Italian named "Faustino" sailed out to Egg Rock to pick forget-me-nots for his sweetheart, a Boston girl named Alice.

Sadly, Faustino never returned from his romantic outing; he perished while trying to get back to shore.

Alice died from the shock of losing her beloved.

A long held legend is that on stormy nights, Alice's ghost returns to the rocks of Nahant and calls out for her lost lover - "Faustino, Faustino!"

A ghost cat naps in the Stephen Daniels House.

STEPHENS DANIELS HOUSE
1 Daniels Street

For over two hundred years the same family owned the 1667 house until Kay Gill bought the place and started to operate the vintage home as a "Bed & Breakfast" long before the concept was in vogue.

In 1953, before she thought of moving to Salem, she painted a portrait of a gray tabby cat. This painting now hangs in the Rose Room. Kay never dreamed that a ghost cat would inhabit this room, or that the feline specter would bear a striking resemblance to the puss in the painting!

Kay admits that she has not witnessed the ghost cat herself, but many of her guests have. She also makes no claims that her place is haunted.

As I stood outside the home snapping photos, two couples emerged who felt *without a doubt* that the place held unseen guests. In fact, the night before one of the men awoke with a start on Halloween Saturday certain there was someone in the room. He picked up his watch and was chilled to the bone when the time and date read: "12:00 AM January 1!"

Who's the female shade peering in the window at the Morning Glory B & B?

MORNING GLORY B & B
22 Hardy Street

The Morning Glory Inn at 22 Hardy Street is an elegant 1808 Georgian Federal style mansion with a spectacular view of Salem Harbor from its rooftop deck. Located directly across from the House of Seven Gables, Bob Shea has owned the inn for about four years and had a story or two to share about his experiences in the antique dwelling.

He received a letter from a guest who was too embarrassed to tell him in person that she saw the apparition of a young woman, about 17 years of age, standing on the balcony outside her room and peering in as if looking for something or someone. Shea has yet to discover the identity or the story of the young shade.

Another time at breakfast a guest asked if the inn was haunted. Before Shea could respond, a teakettle *flew* off the stove and onto the kitchen floor. He simply left the room feeling the guest had received her answer from the source.

Haunted wharf dwelling at Hawthorne Cove Marina.

HAWTHORNE COVE MARINA
10 White Street

Directly across Turner Street from the House of Seven Gables compound is the Hawthorne Cove Marina. It's easy to find. Large boats lie under their protective wraps in the off-season – in the warm cycle, the shipyard bustles with seaside activity.

Robert Ellis Cahill has chronicled New England's folklore in his many books. He has also experienced a few ghosts himself.

In *Haunted Happenings*, Cahill writes about an experience he had with his friend, Mike Purcell. Purcell was interested in purchasing an odd building in the marina and he wanted Cahill's opinion. While Cahill was checking out the structure, he had an encounter with an unfriendly ghost.

The place in question was an unusual summer cottage constructed by Captain Herbert Miller on Salem's waterfront. Miller salvaged an old barge from the harbor that was once owned by a murdered sea captain. He used the hull to add a second story to the wharf dwelling.

As Cahill was looking around the upstairs room he heard a chilling and deep murmur from the barge's pilothouse.

"GET OUT OF HERE!" ordered the disembodied voice. Cahill looked around. *There was no one in the room.*

Was Mike playing a trick on him? He knew the author was into all this ghost stuff, but Cahill couldn't figure it out. What he *did* know was that he was nervous and sweaty, yet at the same time frozen to the spot.

Once again the ominous *"GET OUT OF HERE!"*

Cahill overcame his inertia and raced down the steps passing Purcell on the way. Mike was surprised as the older man ran by him.

"So, what do you think?" he called after him.

"I think the place is haunted," was all Cahill could say.

GRAMPUS
Salem

When it comes to Salem ghost stories, Robert Ellis Cahill seems to be a magnet. This tale involves two of his friends and a boat with a proud history.

The *Grampus* was moored at Salem harbor and there were those seafarers who refused to set foot on her decks. The sight of her gave them the willies!

Her original owner was Frank Quirk who named the vessel *Can Do*, Quirk's philosophy of life learned from his days as a Seabee during World War II.

One winter day an exceptionally fierce snowstorm raged. An oil tanker, named *The Global Hope* went aground on Coney Island Ledge in Salem Sound. Her hull was broken and the engine room was rapidly filling with water. Consequently the ship lost power and radio contact was lost.

The Coast Guard sent out two boats to help the crippled tanker. One had to turn back due to rough seas; the other one radioed that he was lost. Navigational aids were not working right in the near blizzard conditions – 60 mile an hour winds, 20 foot seas and zero visibility.

Enter Frank Quirk. The former Seabee with the "can do" attitude was listening on his radio to this scenario being played out on the rough seas. He was straining at the bit to jump in and help out - and that's just what he did.

Quirk and his crew headed out into the dark seas but unfortunately met with disaster. He radioed that a wave had smashed the ship's windshield and slashed his arm. He shoved a mattress into the broken window, but the boat was taking on water, he was losing a lot of blood, he was weak...then the radio went silent.

A few days later the *Can Do* was found underwater off the Marblehead coast. The bodies of her crew had already washed ashore.

Craig Burnham salvaged the sunken ship and began to repair the damages. While working on the deck he heard voices down in the engine room. He thought it odd - no one else was with him on the boat. He went down to investigate and found nothing. He continued with his welding but when he turned off the torch, he again heard the same noise of a muffled discussion.

Burnham says that whoever inhabits the cabin below can stay there - they bother no one, and the boat is a "can do" ship.

SCHOONER *ANDREW JOHNSON*
Salem

In the 1600s, Salem settlers recorded sporadic sightings of a spectral ship sailing in reverse carrying a man and woman on board. The legend spread that the couple was star-crossed and doomed to sail backwards through life till the end of time.

Another saga of Salem ghosts on the high seas was spawned on March 6, 1869.

The crew on the Schooner *Charles Haskell* was hauling cod aboard the ship in astonishing numbers. In fact one hundred sailing vessels were anchored at Nova Scotia's Georges Bank taking advantage of the fishes' feeding frenzy. One old salt had seen this phenomenon before and the scenario did not bode well. He recalled the last time the fishing was this good...*a terrible wind blew the seas up and a horrible storm wrecked havoc with the ships*.

Sure enough, within hours, severe weather threatened and the captain of the *Charles Haskell* prepared to head home to Gloucester. In fact, all one hundred schooners raced for the safety of the harbor.

By now the storm was a full-blown hurricane. Schooner after schooner swept past the *Haskell* narrowly avoiding a collision.

The *Haskell's* skipper spotted a vessel dead ahead – an accident was inevitable. The *Haskell* smashed into the ill-fated schooner and broke her nearly in half. Then a gigantic wave lifted the *Haskell* and dropped her onto the crippled schooner. All aboard the *Haskell* witnessed the torment of the unfortunate crew as they frantically struggled to keep afloat and stay alive. They begged for help but the *Haskell's* men were helpless in the thrashing seas.

The unknown ship and her crew disappeared forever under the sea. Well, *not exactly...*

Unbelievably, the *Haskell* was unscathed and she made it safely back to port. The incident was reported and it was learned that the unlucky ship was the *Andrew Johnson* out of Salem.

For those who sail the seas, superstition has always ruled the waves. Sailors carried protective charms and amulets such as rings, coins, or stones. They believed their lucky pieces possessed magical powers that could ward off evil and ensure smooth sailing.

But it would take more than their lucky charms to induce eight crewmen to sail with the *Haskell* again. Perhaps they had a premonition of what would transpire two weeks later during a fishing expedition, again to Georges Bank.

The night watchmen dropped their jaws as they observed dripping wet men climbing over the rails and onto the deck. The phantoms stood in the bow and began to bait hooks and tend their fishing lines.

The next day the crew insisted they head back – they refused to sail on the haunted ship - there was no blood on *their* hands.

That night, just after midnight, the undead once again came to life and crawled onto the deck and went about their work as if they were alive. As they approached the harbor, the spirits walked across the water toward Salem.

The *Charles Haskell* never went fishing again, nor did any sailor ever set foot aboard the ship.

The schooner was sold and used as a cargo ship transporting wood.

But chiefly spare, O king of Clouds!
The sailor on his airy shrouds,
When wrecks and beacons strew the steep,
And spectres walk along the deep.

Ode to Winter, T. Campbell. Germany, 1800

Baker's Island Light.
(Photo courtesy of Jeremy D'Entremont)

BAKER'S ISLAND

Five miles off Salem's coast is a chain of fifteen islands that sailors called "The Miseries" evidenced by shipwreck ruins that litter the ocean floor. Poet James Russell Lowell referred to them as "the true isles of the sirens."

Baker's Island is the largest of the dreaded isles, and the only one inhabited. Bordered by sea cliffs, the sound of breaking waves, the squeal of gulls, and the scent of woodsmoke fill the air. Picturesque cottages with wide-open porches dot the pebbled beaches. A stalwart white lighthouse surveys the summer refuge. Blackberry, raspberry, and wild rose bushes abound along with the ferns and tall marsh grass that edge tiny ponds.

Do not be fooled by this bucolic setting. Baker's Island is *very* haunted...

Two light towers were erected on the keeper's house in 1797. Their lights went on January 3, 1798 and were so bright that it is said the first keeper went blind from their glare.

Joseph Perkins was a harbor pilot stationed on the island during the War of 1812. He went to the aid of the *U.S.S. Constitution* when warships were chasing her. He rowed out to the frigate and guided her safely into the harbor.

Perkins was a dedicated pilot who faithfully performed no matter what the weather or risk to his own life. On a particularly foggy night, the sea claimed the dyed-in-the-wool guide while carrying out his duties.

Is it his spirit who still rows to shore splashing his oars in the turbulent surf? There are those who have discerned the specter of an old man dragging a rowboat over the rocks, climbing ashore, but never quite reaching the Old Pilots' house. Built in 1848, this is the oldest structure on the island.

During the winter months the island is literally a ghost town. Only a caretaker is posted on the lonely isle to watch over the vacant homes and maintain the lighthouse and grounds.

Andy Jerome was a previous keeper who eventually went on to become Harbormaster of Danvers. He alleged that the island foghorn was haunted – there could be no other explanation. It seemed to have a mind of its own, blaring at random, even in the most perfect weather.

At every inordinate sounding, Jerome checked the device but determined everything was in good working order. This happened more than a dozen times during his tenure on the island.

The lighthouse was nearly across the 55-acre island from where the horn was housed. When he heard the errant blaring, he would stop what he was doing, walk all the way over to the horn and as he reached the door, the noise would stop. His inspection found nothing wrong. Coast Guard personnel were summoned to repair the horn but they too could find nothing wrong.

This problem with the island's warning devices goes back to the late 1800s when lighthouse keeper, Walter Rogers, had similar frustrations with the fog bell which caused him to leave his post after only two years.

Seventeen years after he retired, Rogers returned to the island for a Fourth of July picnic. As the steamer *Surf City* was leaving the island with her sixty passengers, the fog bell started ringing. Immediately, a waterspout lifted the steamer out of the water and turned her bottoms-up causing her to sink within seconds. Eight people drowned, but Rogers's life was spared.

Ruth Jerome contends that not only the foghorn building, but also the lighthouse and Coast Guard quarters are haunted. Sometimes she observed kerosene lamps aglow in the closed up general store during the dead of winter when no one else was on the island. Ruth definitely sensed a presence and knew that they were not alone.

Who can answer why heavy tools – wrenches, hammers, and ladders seemed to move of their own accord from one place to another. In a matter of minutes, wheelbarrows that were next to the house would be discovered clear across the island. There is no explanation other than the supernatural.

The most chilling incident happened one evening while the Jeromes were making their nightly inspection of all the homes.

When they got to the Chase Cottage, they heard voices, music, and the clinking of glasses. They thought it was the owners' daughters having a party inside the boarded up house.

The couple went up on the porch and knocked on the door. When no one answered, they circled the house until they came to a window that was not boarded. Ruth looked in and saw that the kerosene chandelier was lit and she could see the shadowy movement of people but couldn't recognize who they were.

Thinking they were interlopers, Jerome used his passkey and entered... *they were SHOCKED to find the place empty – not a living soul was inside.* They just could not believe it, and they were utterly spooked.

Previous caretakers also experienced the sounds of levity emanating from the sprawling cottage and the Chase girls themselves admitted to strange happenings in their home when they were children.

One of them awoke at dawn to see a man clad in a khaki green Army jacket standing at the foot of her bed. He was transparent, so she knew right away that he was a ghost.

Living on an island is a unique adventure. People learn out of necessity to "make do, or do without." Therefore, many of the furnishings in the homes on Baker's Island are antique. Think of the many vibrations of times gone by that they retain...

The isolation of Baker's Island life inspires ghost stories. There's one about a horse who died and was buried here. His whinnies are said to fill the still night air.

A jewel thief hiding out on Baker's was captured and jailed in Salem and died behind bars. His specter still searches for the buried booty.

What about the woman who lost her way one summer day and never returned home? In the light of the moon, this bonneted lady in white is still seen trying frantically to find her way her way home.

On the morning of August 20, 1961, avid swimmer and athlete Naomi Colyer went out for her usual morning swim. While in the water, it was her habit to visit the lobstermen boats and sometimes purchase their fresh shellfish for her breakfast. On this day she didn't make it back.

The Coast Guard found her floating on the surface of the water.

The strange thing is *that very night* a resident heard a clunking noise at the island's water pump. He saw a shadow pumping water into a milk can – *the very distinctive container used by Naomi Colyer.* She was the only one on the island who used a milk can to carry water. Subsequent to that sighting, there was several more of the drowned woman seen dripping wet in her bathing suit pumping water.

The Wells Cottage was built in 1896 but the interior reeks of the 1930s. Magazines, canned goods, washing machine – all are vintage. Walking into the Wells Cottage is like walking into a time warp, and that's how the owner liked it.

The house holds more than physical relics. A carpenter hired to do some work in the house bolted from the kitchen because he claimed that a ghost had kissed him fully on the lips!

BEVERLY COVE

Three 17th century homes in Beverly Cove are reputedly haunted. They are all in close proximity to each other and are all part of the estate originally owned by Thomas Lathrop.

Lathrop was a central figure in Essex County - a local hero and revered leader who led a regiment of ardent soldiers in Western Massachusetts. His young troop was known as the "Flower of Essex." Unfortunately, Lathrop's life was cut short in a bloody battle during King Philip's War.

In the 1671 dwelling, phantom pranksters liked to lift the owners' belongings and hide them. When the residents got mad enough and demanded their things back, the objects magically reappeared.

The culprits may be the spirits of two children who supposedly froze to death in front of the fireplace in the 1800s.

Workmen in the house felt as if someone was looking over their shoulder while they worked, and a playful spirit locked one of them in the cellar scaring him silly.

In this same house, the sprite of an elderly woman likes to rock the days away in the living room rocking chair. She's a dear and sweet presence.

The woman of the house thinks the uninvited guest may be the spinster who lived there in the 19th century. According to local historians, the spinster liked to knit. The revenant is especially fond of taking knitting needles and yarn into her nether world until the Mrs. demands them back.

The owners winter in Florida and invited the specter to come with them. Apparently she did just that. Another family joined them as well. One evening their guests' daughter let out a blood-curdling scream. The girl was terribly upset by the vision she had of a woman in a high-collared prairie dress and white bonnet floating in the doorway, her feet inches off the floor.

At the next house on the former Lathrop property, telephones ring off the hook, but when answered, no one is there. This happened constantly and duplicated the ringing experience that occurred in the first house. The sound of imperceptible men walking filled every floor of the old mansion.

This was not a happy house. A malicious and angry presence seemed to permeate the structure.

The third house is a waterfront home and the resident ghost known as "Peter" pushed the owner out the door trying to keep him from entering on moving day.

The old servant bells rang incessantly so they had to be disconnected. Then the motion detector kept on going off for no reason (or was it detecting an unseen predator?).

The most bizarre event was when water poured from the kitchen ceiling and walls. When plumbers were called in, they could not detect a problem nor find the source of the water

None other than Robert Ellis Cahill's daughter was a tenant in the house and witnessed the paranormal phenomena.

One night she awakened to the sound of papers rustling on her bookshelf. She saw the balled up paper she had tossed in the garbage earlier, move along the top of a bookshelf. She yelled at the pesky spook to stop scaring her – she had had enough already! With that, her pile of schoolbooks lifted off the desk and fell to the floor with a thud.

These three homes continue their 300-year-old connection into the millennium linked by mysterious happenings within their walls.

MARBLEHEAD COASTLINE

The charming village of Marblehead lies across Salem Bay and was the backdrop for a brutal attack by buccaneers in the late 1600s.

The legend is that Spanish pirates commandeered a vessel and robbed all aboard of their valuables. They took one prisoner – a British woman. They stole all her jewelry except for a beautiful emerald ring that remained stuck on her finger. All in her traveling party were murdered, but she was held captive, likely for the bounty stuck on her finger.

They brought her back to the ship to see if one of their comrades could remove the ring, but to no avail. They sailed to Marblehead with the intent to maraud the tiny fishing village and the pirates took their hostage to the mainland.

Now that she was on *firma terra*, the woman tried to escape. A tragic mistake. For a while she ran free, but she was recaptured.

The looters failed to get hold of the treasures they expected. Now they were *really* angry.

They took their anger out on the poor woman. She was brutally beat and stabbed, and finally off came her finger. The jewel was theirs! The savages left the wounded woman on the beach in a bloody heap.

Marblehead fisherman and their families heard her cries and screams for help, but they were too frightened to come to her aid. They remained huddled in their hiding places.

As the pirates sailed away from the coastal town and faded in the distance, the battered woman breathed her last breath.

The fishermen were sympathetic, and now that they were out of harm's way, they could help. As a kind gesture, they buried her broken body.

If you want to sample the terror of this long ago torture, take a stroll along Screeching Lady Beach off Front Street. As the name implies, they say that in the dead of night, or at dawn's first light, if you listen closely enough, the terrible screams of the English lady can still be heard…

LA BELLE STUART
Newburyport

Millions of tourists travel to the North Shore's scenic seaside towns every year. One royal lady in particular was known to frequent Newburyport often so that she could spend time with her son. Her love for him was so strong that she overcame the constraints of death and traveled in spirit from beyond the grave.

In the 17th century during the reign of Charles II, La Belle Stuart, celebrated Duchess of Richmond and Lennox, was the toast of London. Aptly named, her beauty was legendary and in 1692 she modeled for the figure of Britannia on a copper halfpenny. Her embossed likeness insured her physical image lived on in perpetuity and Stuart's ephemeral self lived on as well - long after her death.

Her tiny oval portrait and a small bejeweled filigree chest containing love letters were found hidden behind the wainscoting in a Newburyport room occupied by Jeremy Probart. The letters were cryptically signed "L.L.," which stood for "Lennox Love," La Belle Stuart's noted signature to intimates.

The special silver box was a gift from King Charles II and it is now displayed in the National Gallery of Edinburgh.

History reveals that Stuart had many lovers, but her favorite by far was her cousin Lord Blantyre. Her "dearest Trassie" was her constant companion for many years.

When Blantyre fell out of favor with the King, Stuart used all her savings to purchase a castle for her dejected cousin. The ivy covered, turreted castle bore the romantic name "Lennoxlove."

Jeremy Probart arrived on the packet ship *Aurora Borealis* on a windswept September day in 1701. The town folk came out to see the largest ship ever to berth at the Newburyport wharf. The captain had been blown off course and struggled in the stormy seas to deposit his special passenger.

Arrangements had been made months before by a Newburyport banker, Mr. Dalrymple, and the Dean of Galloway College, near the Firth of Forth in Scotland, to secret the young man to America.

Political tension in Scotland was at an all time high, so for the young man's protection he was sent to the New World to work as a schoolmaster. He would reside in the home of Mistress Deborah Caswell.

Concealed in his cloak was a treasured possession bequeathed to him by his great aunt. A small embellished casket containing letters from his mother to his father, and a tiny portrait of his mother painted on wood.

Having lived in foster homes much of his life, he cherished the time he spent alone in his room reading the love letters; this was how he came to know his parents.

Of his fondest memories was the time he spent with his Great Aunt Gordon-Lennox. He often remembered the magical evening when a beautiful woman came to visit him there. She sailed into the room and swept him into her arms, her great plumed hat nearly suffocating him. He sat at her feet mesmerized by her radiance and the affection she bestowed on him. Her identity was never revealed, but everyone in the room referred to her as "Your Grace."

One evening as Mistress Deborah entered Jeremy's room to prepare his bed, she saw a woman dressed in satin sitting in a chair by the fireplace gently rocking a cradle with her foot. At one point the bejeweled woman leaned over the cradle and smiled at the sleeping baby. She then put a finger to her lips and disappeared into the shadows.

When Mistress Deborah told Jeremy about her sighting of the apparition, he was not the least bit disturbed. Previously, when he sat in his room at night working on his poetry or school papers, he often heard a woman's voice calling him by name and the sound of her rustling skirts on the floorboards.

"I think I know the meaning of these visitations," said Jeremy.

Before he left Scotland, Jeremy made sure he paid a visit to his Great Aunt Gordon-Lennox. She had given him the small chest containing the five letters sealed with "L.L."

She told him to ask her no questions because she was held to a promise. Her advice was for him to read the five letters, and to read *between* the lines, for then he would know his mother and his father. The letters opened with "Dearest Trassie."

In the night, Jeremy heard the whispers and the floorboards squeak and the sound of rustling satin in his room. He too came to see the regal woman rocking the cradle and smiling at the invisible baby.

One day a long-awaited letter arrived from the Dean of Galloway in answer to one Jeremy had written. Yes, Her Grace the Duchess of Richmond and Lennox had died over two years ago.

Jeremy sought out Mistress Caswell to share with her that he at last was certain who was haunting his room. The woman was his mother, La Belle Stuart.

Many years later after Jeremy's death when the room was being refurbished, the small chest of letters and the tiny portrait on wood were found behind the paneling.

A son of Mr. Dalrymple, the Newburyport banker, took the portrait and the letters to Scotland where they repose among the other Stuart treasures at Castle Lennoxlove.

THE GARRISON INN
Newburyport

Celebrated as the birthplace of the U. S. Coast Guard, Newburyport rivaled Boston as the nation's shipbuilding and trade center during the 1600s.

Strangely enough, the remnants of an underground world exist beneath this historic town.

Subterranean tunnels meander beneath Newburyport's streets and were discovered when a parking lot collapsed behind State Street. Some believe these brick burrows were built for smuggling goods in order to avoid British import taxes.

Others feel they are leftover slave tunnels constructed along the Underground Railroad.

Newburyport was a strong abolitionist town thanks to the city's most famous resident, William Lloyd Garrison, the father of the anti-slave movement.

The network of tunnels is extensive and nearly a city in itself connecting door to door the many mansions and establishments above.

The labyrinth is reputedly haunted because of the moans and cries heard issuing from the boarded up entrances to the tunnels in people's basements.

The Garrison Inn, a National Registered Historic Landmark, is named after the man who devoted himself to ending slavery. The 19th century manse retains its original brick walls and hand hewn wooden beams.

In the cellar, an underground entrance to the mysterious tunnels also exists. When the building was renovated to serve as an inn in the early 1900s, spooky beings emerged from this cavern.

The wraiths of ragged waifs manifested and seemed to be begging for a handout as they huddled in the shadows.

Captain Moses Brown was the original owner of the 1809 mansion. Brown was a tradesman who imported molasses and sold it to the rum distilleries.

He was also a noted philanthropist, renowned for his generosity and refusing no one. Could it be these poor phantoms are still playing out their earthly existence as paupers, turning to the kind man for help?

When he died in 1827, he bequeathed the home to his sister Sarah White Bannister. She died in the house in 1880, but according to those who have encountered her apparition, Sarah has not yet left her mortal abode.

Her form in a flowing white gown is usually spotted in front of the basement fireplace, but once she shadowed a guest while he was signing the register. The terrified desk clerk spotted the specter floating in the air, but managed to keep her composure lest she lose a paying customer!

The most frequently sighted ghost is an Abe Lincoln look alike complete with stove top hat.

Reportedly the specters of three slaves still linger where perhaps they once sought refuge in this abolition capital.

Most of the unearthly activity arises from beneath the ground in this distinguished double-decker town.

*"Then a spirit passed before my face;
the hair of my flesh stood up."*

Book of Job 4:15

JUST A FEW MORE...

Ghosts are everywhere and not all of them are linked to historic places or events. Salem has her fair share of "everyday" ghosts as well.

In *GHOSTS, True Encounters with the World Beyond*, Hans Holzer relates the story of a Salem woman whose grandmother had passed. Her grandfather was lost without his life partner and soon left this world for the next.

At the funeral parlor, the Salem woman had the distinct feeling that someone was watching her. When she looked up, the apparitions of her grandparents were standing over the coffin and smiling. They telepathically conveyed the message that they were happy to be reunited in the afterlife.

According to Dennis William Hauck (*Haunted Places, The National Directory*), the ghost of a woman who died giving birth at Salem Hospital has been seen by doctors and nurses in the hallways while at the Salem YMCA, many lifeguards at the pool see shady movements and hear noises by the stairwell leading to the old pool. Rumor has it that someone drowned there and their spirit remains.

ACKNOWLEDGEMENTS

I'd like to express my appreciation to the following individuals for their assistance...

Jeremy D'Entremont of Coastlore Productions for his beautiful photo of Baker's Island Lighthouse. Visit his website - *New England Lighthouses: A Virtual Guide* at www.lighthouse.cc

John Wall of the Salem Inn who has heard from guests that they *"hear strange noises and see doors open and close on their own"* at the inn, but John and his co-workers feel this is just the *"spirit of Salem"* stimulating their imaginations.

And for their stories...

"Kay," Joseph Edwards House.
Kay Gill of The Stephens Daniels House.
Carol Manley, Public Relations Director, Hawthorne Hotel.
Bob Shea of the Morning Glory B & B.

BIBLIOGRAPHY

Barraco, Bob, "An Old New England Haunting." *GHOST TRACKERS NEWSLETTER*, Vol. 9 No. 3, October 1990.

_____, "The Sighing Ghost of Carpenter Street." *GHOST TRACKERS NEWSLETTER*, Vol. 8 No. 2, June 1989.

Cahill, Robert Ellis, *Haunted Happenings*. Old Saltbox Publishing House, Inc., Salem, MA; 1992.

_____, *New England's Things That Go Bump In The Night*. Chandler-Smith Publishing House, Inc., Peabody, MA; 1983.

_____, *Ghostly Haunts*. Chandler-Smith Publishing House, Inc., Peabody, MA; 1983.

_____, *New England's Witches and Wizards*. Chandler-Smith Publishing House, Inc., Peabody, MA; 1983.

Editors, *USA Weekend, I Never Believed in Ghosts Until....* Contemporary Books, Chicago, IL; 1992.

Hauck, Dennis William, *Haunted Places, The International Directory*. Penguin Books, New York, NY; 1994.

Holzer, Hans, *GHOSTS, True Encounters with the World Beyond*. Black Dog & Levanthal Publishers, Inc., New York, NY; 1997.

Myers, Arthur, *The Ghostly Register.* Contemporary Books, Chicago, IL; 1986.

Reynolds, James, *Ghosts in American Houses.* Paperback Library, New York, NY; 1955.

Schensul, Jill, "Salem, dead on." *The Bergen Record,* Ramsey, NJ; October 10, 1999.

Snow, Edward Rowe, *Fantastic Folklore and Fact.* Dodd, Mead & Co., New York, NY; 1968.

_____, *Strange Tales from Nova Scotia to Cape Hatteras.* Dodd, Mead & Co., New York, NY; 1949.

Thompson, William O., *The Dead Still Whisper, New England Ghosts.* Old Saltbox Publishing, Salem, MA; 2000.

The following Internet websites were also referenced:

House of Seven Gables: www.7gables.org

National Park Service: www.nps.gov/sama

New England Lighthouses: www.lighthouse.cc

Salem City Guide: www.salemweb.com

HAUNTED SALEM GHOST TOURS

Haunted Footsteps Ghost Tour
8 Derby Square
978-745-0666

"Into the DEAD of the Night"
Salem's Original Ghost Walk
www.theflagship.net

Mass. Hysteria Haunted Hearse Tours®
1-877-4-HEARSE (1-877-443-2773)
"It's a grave undertaking."™

Salem's Harrowing Ghostly Tours
282 – 288 Derby Street
978-740-2929

Spellbound Tours
www.spellboundtours.com
978-745-0138

Other Books By

Lynda Lee Macken

GHOSTS OF THE GARDEN STATE

ADIRONDACK GHOSTS

HAUNTED HISTORY OF STATEN ISLAND

For purchasing information, please contact the publisher:

BLACK CAT PRESS
Post Office Box 1218
Forked River, NJ 08731
609-971-9334
llmacken@hotmail.com

Quantity discounts are available on bulk purchases.

THE END